GUNS N' ROSES
USE YOUR ILLUSION I

ROBERT JOHN

Management: Doug Goldstein/
Big F D Entertainment, Inc.
Edited by Jon Chappell, Steve Gorenberg
and Kerry O'Brien
Music Engraving by W.R. Music
Production Manager: Daniel Rosenbaum
Art Direction: Kerstin Fairbend
Director Of Music: Mark Phillips

Cover Painting: Mark Kostabi

ISBN:0-89524-683-X

GENE KIRKLAND

Contents

RIGHT NEXT DOOR TO HELL

**Words and Music by
Izzy Stradlin', Timo Caltia
and W. Axl Rose**

Right next door to hell, _____ got no-where else __ to be. __

Right next door to hell, ____ feels like the walls are clos-ing in on __ me.

Fuck you, ____

2. My

bitch!

Not bad kids, just stu - pid ones.__ Yeah, thought we'd own the world an get - tin' used was hav - in' fun. I said we're

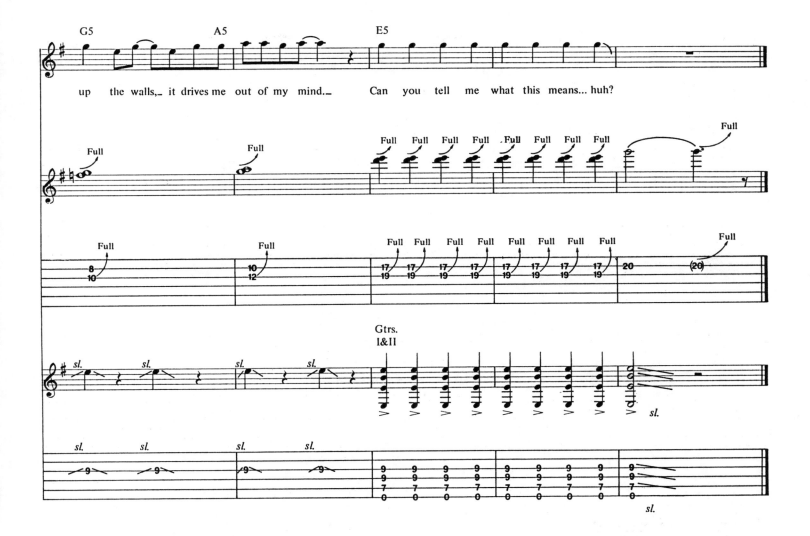

up the walls,_ it drives me out of my mind._ Can you tell me what this means... huh?

Additional Lyrics

2. My mama never really said much to me,
   She was much too young and scared ta be.
   Hell, "Freud" might say that's what I need,
   But all I really ever get is greed.
   An most my friends, they feel the same.
   Hell, we don't even have ourselves to blame.
   But times are hard and thrills are cheaper.
   As your arms get shorter, your pockets get deeper.

2nd Chorus:
Right next door to hell.
Why don't you write a letter to me?
I said I'm right next door to hell,
An so many eyes are on me.
Right next door to hell,
I never thought this is where I'd be.
But I'm right next door to hell,
Thinkin' time'll stand still for me. *(To Guitar solo)*

DUST N' BONES

Words and Music by
Izzy Stradlin', Duff McKagan
and Slash

1. She loved him yes - ter - day.__ Yes - ter - day's o -
2. *See additional lyrics*

*Play B (⑤ 2fr.) 1st time only.

ver, I__ said o - kay, that's all right.__

(end Riff A)

(end Rhy. Fig. 1)

(Yeah, ___ ow ___ yeah.) ___

Ya get out _ on your own. ___ And you take all _ that you own. ___ And you
(Yeah.) ___

for - get a - bout your home. ___ And then you're just fuck - in' gone! ___

*Mute w/edge of pick, creating a semi - harmonic.

Additional Lyrics

2. She loved him yesterday.
He laid her sister, she said O.K.
An that's all right.
Buried her things today
Way back out deep behind the driveway.
And that's all right.

2nd Chorus:
Sometimes these women are so easy.
Sometimes these women are so cold.
Sometimes these women seem to rip you right in two,
Only if you let 'em get to you. *(To Bridge)*

LIVE AND LET DIE

Words and Music by
Paul McCartney and Linda McCartney

DON'T CRY (ORIGINAL)

Words and Music by
Izzy Stradlin' and W. Axl Rose

*Lead vocal doubled one octave higher (till Guitar solo).

Don't you cry_____ to-night. There's a heav-en a-bove____ you, ba - by.
Ooh._____ Ooh.)_____

2nd Verse
w/Fill 2

And don't you cry_____ to - night.____

(cont. in slashes)

Give me a whis-per,

Fill 2

Gtr. II

clean tone w/echo
p

28

*Play only lowest note of chord when P.M.
is indicated (throughout).

Fdbk. pitch.: A

*Vib. applies to bottom note only.

3rd Verse
w/Fill 3

And please re - mem - ber   that I nev - er___ lied.___

*Lead vocal doubled one octave
higher (next 2 bars).

Fill 3

Don't you cry to-night.

Fill 5

*Swell w/vol. control.

PERFECT CRIME

Words and Music by
Izzy Stradlin', Slash
and W. Axl Rose

1st Verse
w/Rhy. Figs. 1 & 1A
N.C.(Am)

1. Kick - in' back___ in the shad - ows.   Got   no   need___ for the light.___

___   Who's   sor - ry   now,_____   old   tim - er?   Look   at   how___   you've

(G#5)(A5)(A#5)   N.C.(Bm)

spent   your___ life._____   Scroung - in'   for change__ to put some mon-ey   in   your   pock -et.   My, how scratch___ does

burn.   Laugh - in'   at   the   suck - ers   as   you pissed it   a - way.___   2. But

B5   C5   C#5   D5   D#5   E5

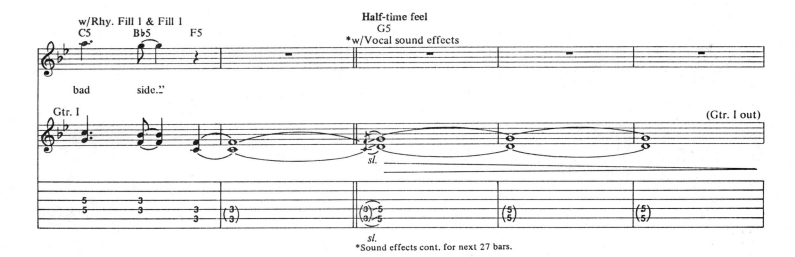

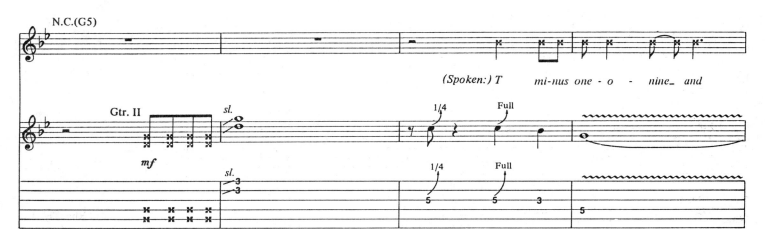

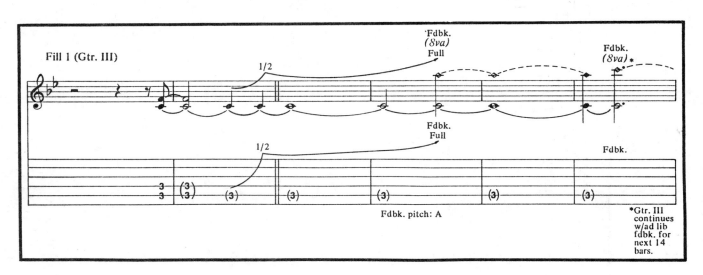

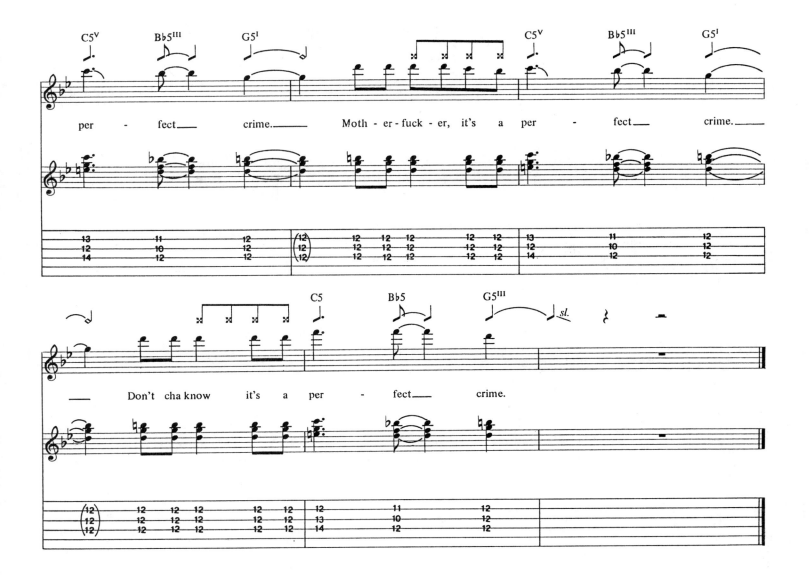

Additional Lyrics

3. Call on everybody who's got last rites.
   Said, "It's better if you locked 'em away."
   Runnin' through the visions
   At the speed of light.

   3rd Chorus:
   Won't ya let me be?
   Motherfucker, just let me be.
   Goddamn it, better let me be.
   Don't ya know ya better let me be, *etc.*

YOU AIN'T THE FIRST

Words and Music by
Izzy Stradlin'

in the dark, was-n't meant to last____ long.
rar - y lov - er, hon-ey, you ain't the first.

I think you've worn your wel - come,
Lots of oth - ers came be -

hon - ey, I'll just sing you a - long.
fore you, wom-an, said, but you been the worst.

As I sing you this
Sa'

song.

One, two, three, one.

you've been the worst.__

Two three and. So

Deep down in - side.

steady gliss.

Begin fade

Fade out

50

BAD OBSESSION

Words and Music by
Izzy Stradlin' and West Arkeen

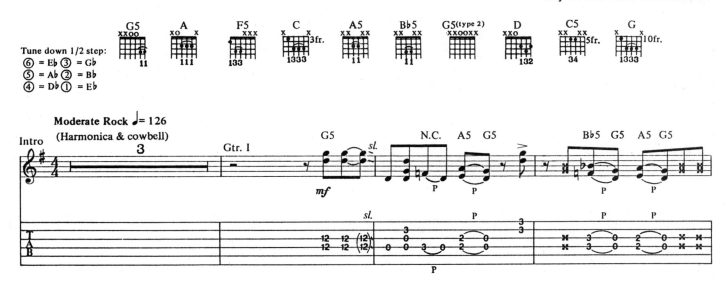

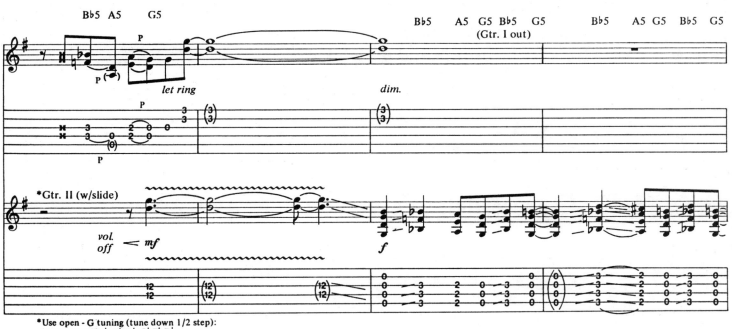

*Use open - G tuning (tune down 1/2 step):
(low to high) Db Gb Db Db Gb Bb Db

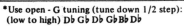

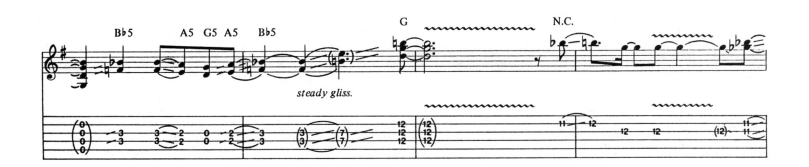

1. I can't stop think-in', think-in' 'bout sink-in', sink-in' down in-to my bed._

2. *See additional lyrics*

I call my moth-er, she's just a cunt_ now. She said I'm sick in the head._

She said, "You ain't spe-cial, so who you fool-in'? Don't try ta give me a line."_

w/Rhy. Fig. 4 (2 times)

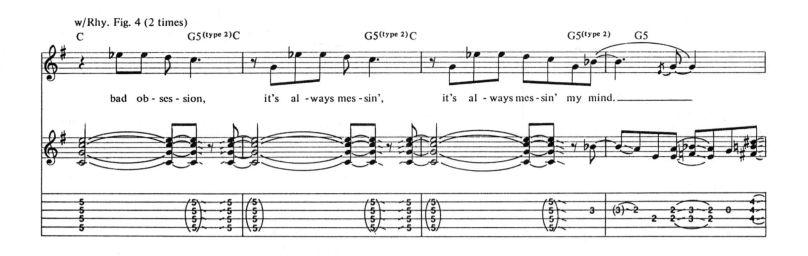

bad ob - ses - sion, it's al -ways mes - sin', it's al -ways mes-sin' my mind._____

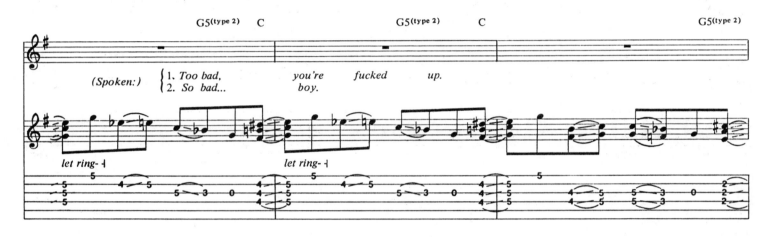

(Spoken:) 1. Too bad, you're fucked up.
2. So bad... boy.

w/Rhy. Fig. 4 (1st 3 bars only)

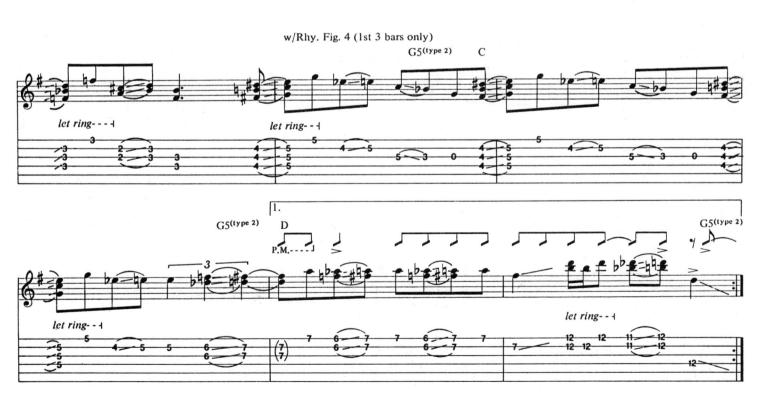

*TAB numbers are imaginary fret
numbers past the fingerboard.

Additional Lyrics

2. I used to be wasted, always tried to take it,
   Take it down into my vein.
   I call the doctor, he's just another,
   He said I'm sick in the brain.
   He said, "You ain't special, so who you foolin'?
   Don't try ta give me a line."
   But I can't stop thinking 'bout doin' it one more time. (Oh no.)
   But I already left you and you're better off left behind. (Oh yeah.) *(To Chorus)*

BACK OFF BITCH

Words and Music by
Paul Huge, W. Axl Rose,
Chris Weber and Slash

59

When you feel the fi - re,_____ wo - o - o - oh,_____   and taste the flame,

Back off,_ back off bitch._ Down in the gut - tar, dy - in' in the ditch. You bet - ter

yeah.

Back off,_____ back off_ bitch, bitch, bitch, bitch, bitch.

(Spoken:) Hey wha'd'ya think he's tryin' to say there, anyway?

I think it's something each person's s'posed to take in their own special way.   Fuck-ing bitch!
(Fucking bitch!)

DOUBLE TALKIN' JIVE

Words and Music by
Izzy Stradlin'

NOVEMBER RAIN

Words and Music by
W. Axl Rose

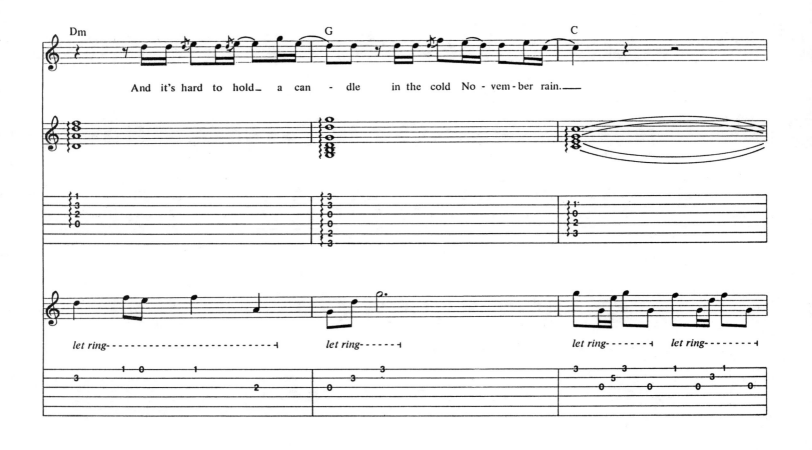

And it's hard to hold_ a can - dle in the cold No - vem - ber rain._

let ring- - - - - - - - - - - - - - - -   *let ring- - - - - -*   *let ring- - - - - - -*   *let ring- - - - - - -*

We've been through this_ such a long,_ long_ time just try - in' to kill_ the pain._

let ring- - - - -

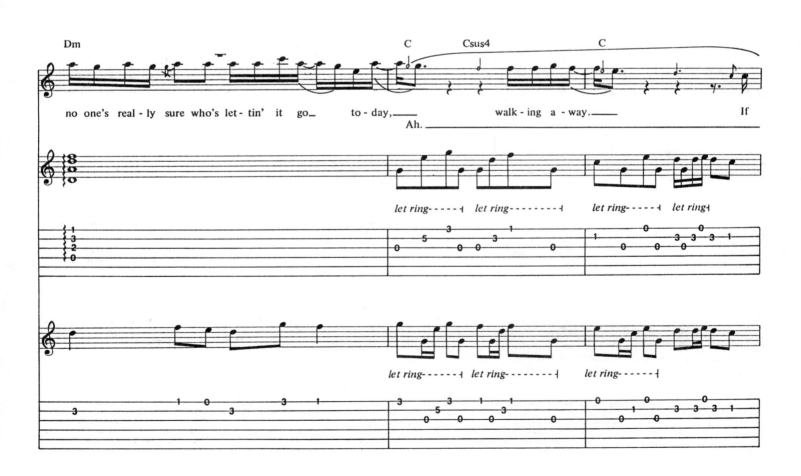

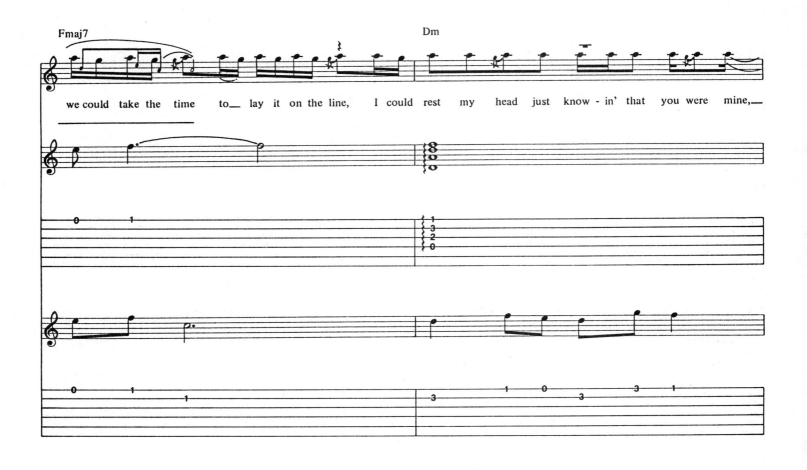

we could take the time to__ lay it on the line, I could rest my head just know - in' that you were mine,__

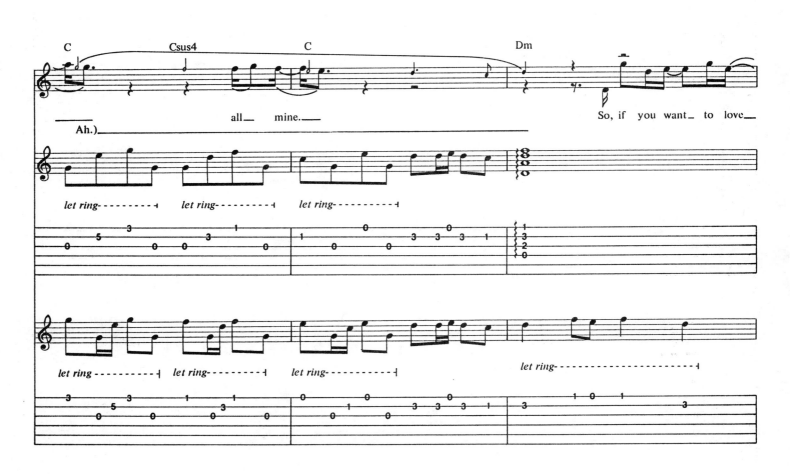

all__ mine.__
Ah.)__

So, if you want__ to love__

And when your fears_ sub-side_____ and shad-ows still_ re-main,_ oh_ yeah,_

(Ah._____

I know that you_ can love_ me when there's no one left to blame._

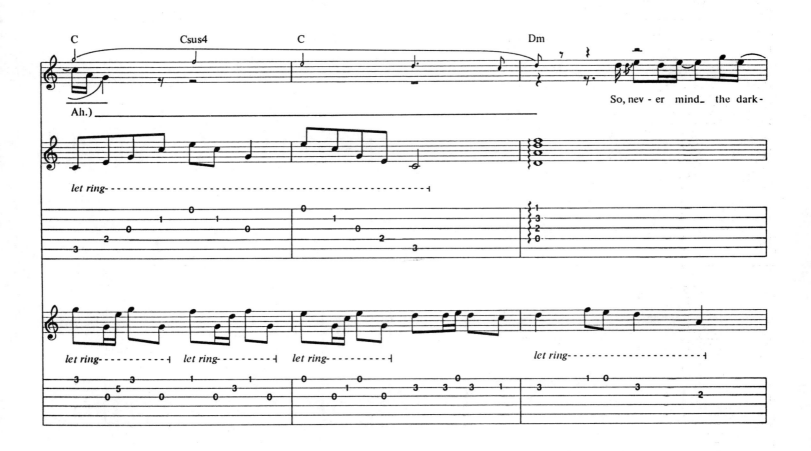

Ah.)

So, nev - er mind_ the dark-

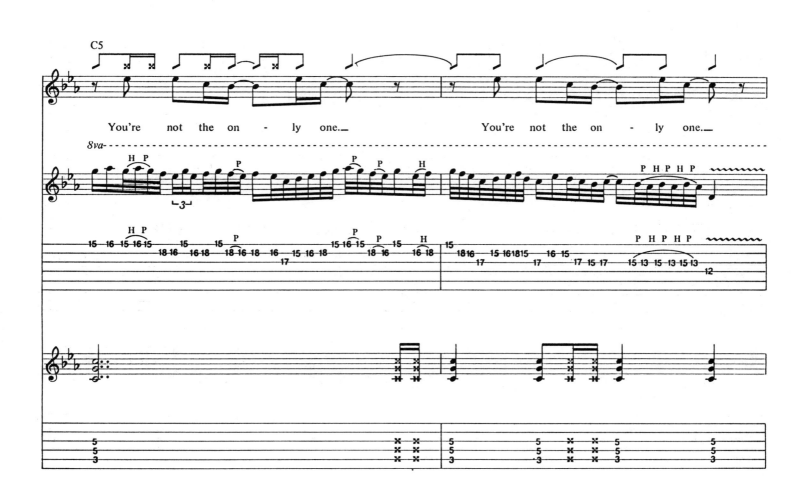

You're not the on - ly one.___ You're not the on - ly one.___

(cont. in slashes)

Don't ya think that you need some-bod-y? Don't ya think that you need some-one? Ev -'ry-bod-y needs_ some-bod-y.

THE GARDEN

Words and Music by
West Arkeen, Del James
and W. Axl Rose

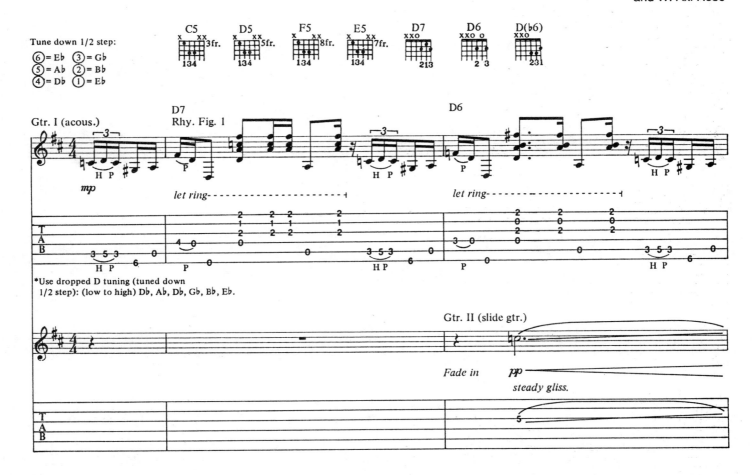

*Use dropped D tuning (tuned down
1/2 step): (low to high) Db, Ab, Db, Gb, Bb, Eb.

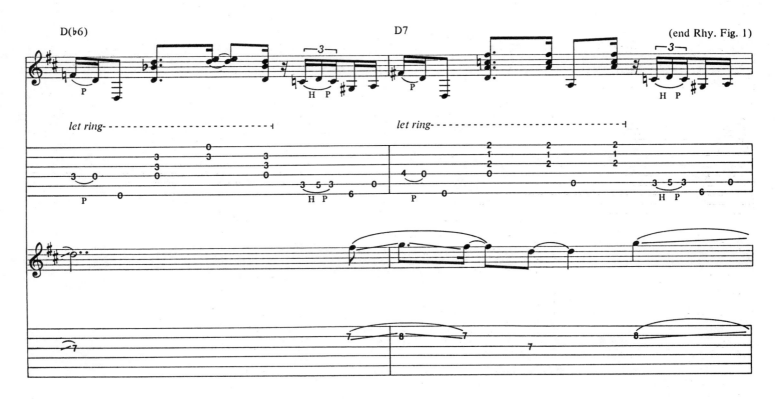

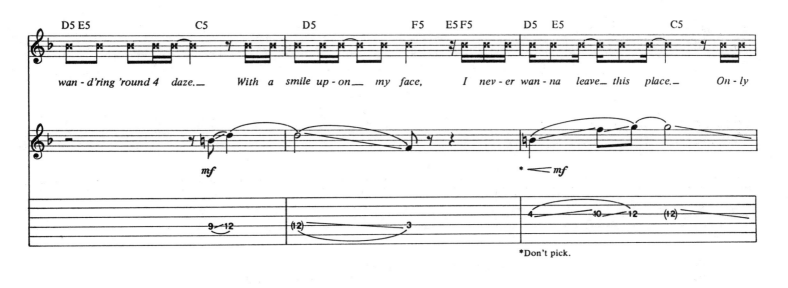

wan - d'ring 'round 4 daze.__ With a smile up - on__ my face, I nev - er wan - na leave__ this place.__ On - ly

*Don't pick.

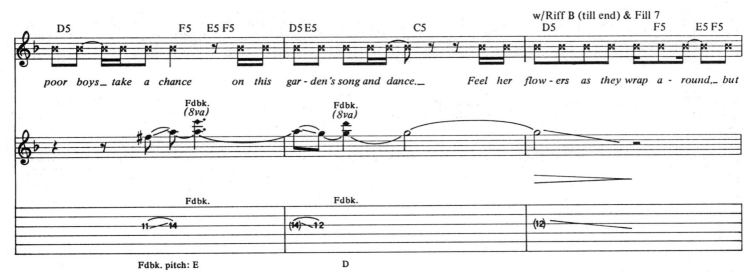

w/Riff B (till end) & Fill 7

poor boys__ take a chance on this gar - den's song and dance.__ Feel her flow - ers as they wrap a - round,__ but

Fdbk. pitch: E   D

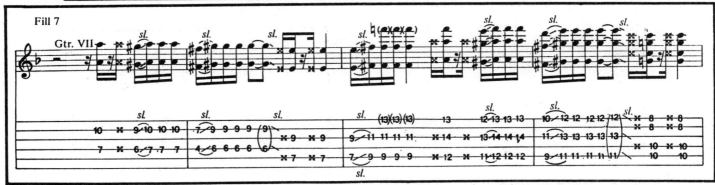

on - ly smart boys do with - out. Turned in - to my___ worst pho - bi - a, it's a cra - zy man's___ u - to - pi - a. If you're

lost no one can show ya, but it sure was glad to know___ ya. Bye, bye.___ So long.___ Bye,

Riff C

Fill 8

*Strum behind nut.

104

GARDEN OF EDEN

Words and Music by
Slash and W. Axl Rose

run - nin' round   back,   see 'em line   up   on their knees. 'Cause the kiss ass syc - o - phants throw - in'

pen - ance   at   your feet. When they got   no - where   to   go,   watch 'em come   in   off   the streets.   While they're

bang - in'   out   front, in - side they're slam - min' to   the crunch. Go   on   an throw me   to   the li - ons and the

whole damn scream - in'   bunch._ 'Cause the   pissed - off__   rip - offs 'r' ev - 'ry - where you   turn.

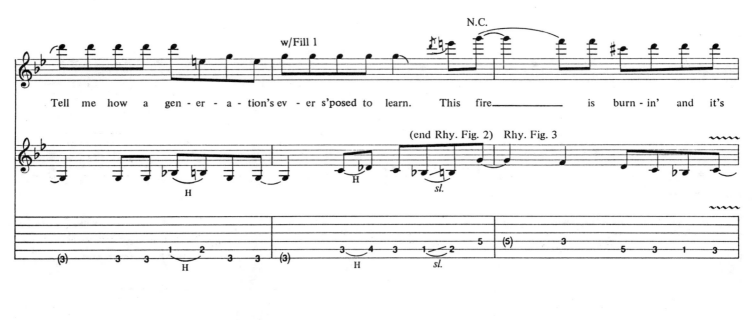

Tell me how a gen - er - a - tion's ev - er s'posed to learn. This fire_____ is burn - in' and it's

out of con - trol.__ It's not a - prob - lem you can stop. It's rock n' roll.__

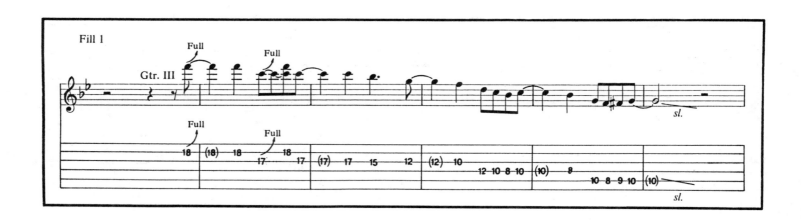

2nd, 3rd Verses
w/Rhy. Fig. 1 (3½ times - both gtrs.)

Gb5 F5 E5

G5   E5

2. I   read it on a   wall, it went
3. Look - ing through this

(end Rhy. Fig. 4)

A5   G5 G#5 E5   G5   E5   A5   G5 G#5 E5

straight   to   my head. It said, "Dance   to   the ten - sion of   a   world__ on   edge." We got
point   of   view,__ there's no   way I'm   gon - na   fit in.__

G5   E5   A5   G5 G#5 E5   G5   E5

ra - cial   vi - 'lence,   and who'll cast   the first   stone. And sex   is   used__ an - y -
Don't ya tell   me what   my eyes   see.__   Don't ya tell   me who__ to be - lieve__

109

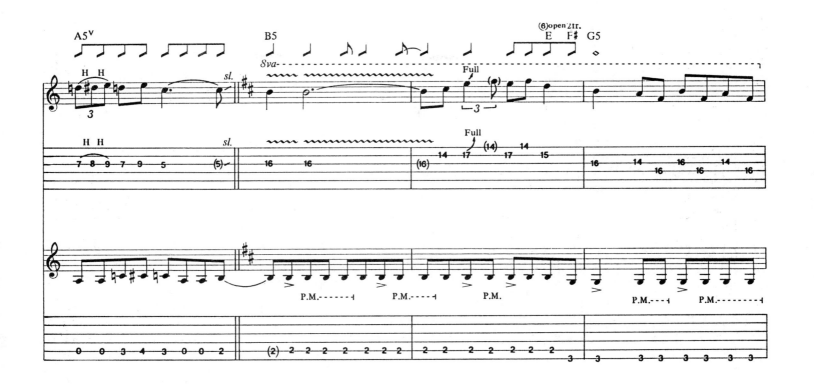

(Spoken:) An we ain't talking about no poison apple or some

den. Said we're lost ___ in the Gar-den of E den. Said there's no___

___ one's gon-na be-lieve_____ this. But we're lost___ in the Gar-den of E-

missin' rib, ya hear?

N.C. w/Rhy. Fig. 3 (Gtrs. I & II)

den. This fire_____ is burn-in' and it's out of con-trol.___ It's not a

Gtrs. I & II

prob-lem you can stop. It's rock n' roll.___

A.H. (8va)

A.H.

DON'T DAMN ME

Words and Music by
Slash, Dave Lank
and W. Axl Rose

(Gtrs. I & II cont. in notation)

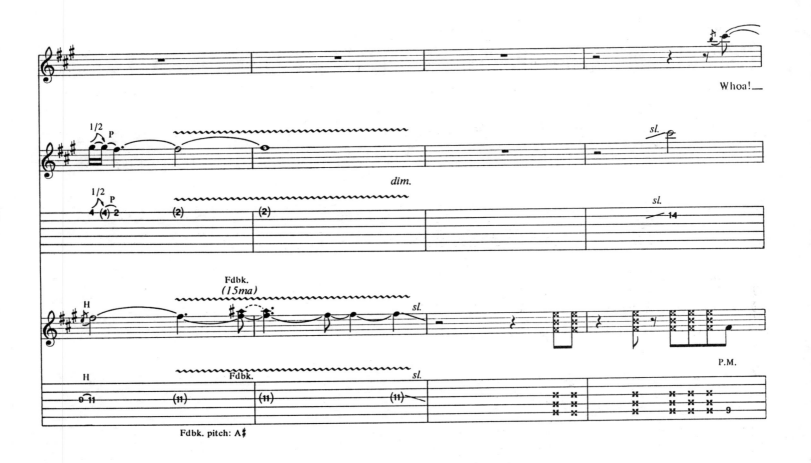

Whoa!___

dim.

Fdbk. pitch: A♯

F♯5

Don't___

(Gtr. II cont. in Rhy. Fig. 1)

(Spoken:) Smoke 'em if ya got 'em!

*C sounded by vibrato; pull offs
caused by pulling E stg. off neck.

All right! That sucked!

A.H. pitch: B

BAD APPLES

Words and Music by
Slash, Duff McKagan,
Izzy Stradlin' and W. Axl Rose

DEAD HORSE

Words and Music by
W. Axl Rose

(Spoken:) Then when she said she was gonna like wreck my car, I didn't know what to do.   Woh!_____

Tag
w/Rhy. Fig. 1 (Acous. gtr.)

Sick of this life,___ not that you'd care.___

I'm not the on — ly one___ with whom these feel - ings I share.___

COMA

Words and Music by
Slash and W. Axl Rose

ev - er come back to this world a - gain.

Kind-a like it in a co - ma 'cause no one's ev - er gon - na,

oh,   make me   come_   back   to_   this   world   a - gain_

_____   Now   I   feel   as   if   I'm   float - ing   a - way._   I   can't   feel_

Gtr. III

P.M.---------------------------------
w/flanger

_____ all   the   pres - sure   and   I   like   it   this   way,_   but   my   bod - y's   call - in',   my   bod-

P.M.---------------------------------

y's call - in'. Won't ya come__ back to__ this

world a - gain?_____ Sus - pend - ed deep in a sea__

(Gtr. III)

P.M.-------------------------------

w/flanger

of black,__ I've got the light at the end. I've got the bones on the mast._ Well, I've

__ gone sail - in', I've__ gone sail - in'.   I could leave so eas-

(cont. in notation)

(Gtr. III out)

Gtrs. I & II

P.M.

No one's gon-na both-er me an - y - more.___ No one's gon - na mess with my

head no more.___ I can't un-der-stand___ what all the fight - in's for,

but it's so___ nice___ here down off the shore.

wish you could see__ this 'cause there's noth-ing to see.__ It's peace-ful here__ and it's fine__

__ with me.__ Not like the world__ where I used__ to live.__

I nev-er real-ly wan-ted to live.__

Ah.__

much for con-so-la-tion when you feel___ so weak and old.___ But if home___ is where the heart___ is, then there's

sto-ries to be told.___ No, you don't need no doc-tor. No one else___ can heal your soul. Got your mind___

___ in sub-mis-sion, got your life on the line.___ But no-bod-y pulled the trig-ger, they just

*Play only lowest note of chord (muted) when muted stg. is indicated (till end).

stepped a-side.___ They be down___ by the wa-ter while you watch 'em wav-ing good-bye.___

gon - na take some time t'heal__ the bro - ken mem -'ries that an - oth - er man would need just to sur -

vive._____

TABLATURE EXPLANATION

TABLATURE: A six-line staff that graphically represents the guitar fingerboard, with the top line indicating the highest sounding string (high E). By placing a number on the appropriate line, the string and fret of any note can be indicated. The number 0 represents an open string.

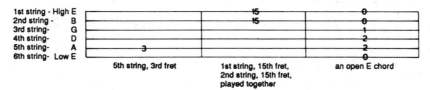

1st string - High E
2nd string - B
3rd string - G
4th string - D
5th string - A
6th string - Low E

5th string, 3rd fret

1st string, 15th fret,
2nd string, 15th fret,
played together

an open E chord

Definitions for Special Guitar Notation

BEND: Strike the note and bend up ½ step (one fret).

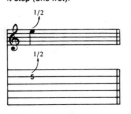

BEND: Strike the note and bend up a whole step (two frets).

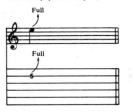

BEND AND RELEASE: Strike the note and bend up ½ (or whole) step, then release the bend back to the original note. All three notes are tied, only the first note is struck.

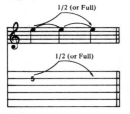

PRE-BEND: Bend the note up ½ (or whole) step, then strike it.

PRE-BEND AND RELEASE: Bend the note up ½ (or whole) step. Strike it and release the bend back to the original note.

UNISON BEND: Strike the two notes simultaneously and bend the lower note up to the pitch of the higher.

VIBRATO: The string is vibrated by rapidly bending and releasing the note with the left hand or tremolo bar.

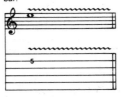

WIDE OR EXAGGERATED VIBRATO: The pitch is varied to a greater degree by vibrating with the left hand or tremolo bar.

SLIDE: Strike the first note and then slide the same left-hand finger up or down to the second note. The second note is not struck.

SLIDE: Same as above, except the second note is struck.

HAMMER-ON: Strike the first (lower) note, then sound the higher note with another finger by fretting it without picking.

PULL-OFF: Place both fingers on the notes to be sounded. Strike the first note and without picking, pull the finger off to sound the second (lower) note.

TRILL: Very rapidly alternate between the note indicated and the small note shown in parentheses by hammering on and pulling off.

TAPPING: Hammer ("tap") the fret indicated with the right-hand index or middle finger and pull off to the note fretted by the left hand.

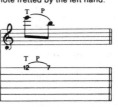

PICK SLIDE: The edge of the pick is rubbed down the length of the string producing a scratchy sound.

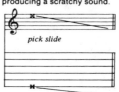

pick slide

TREMOLO PICKING: The note is picked as rapidly and continuously as possible.

trem. pick

NATURAL HARMONIC: Strike the note while the left hand lightly touches the string over the fret indicated.

ARTIFICIAL HARMONIC: The note is fretted normally and a harmonic is produced by adding the edge of the thumb or the tip of the index finger of the right hand to the normal pick attack. High volume or distortion will allow for a greater variety of harmonics.

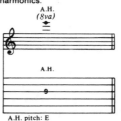

A.H. pitch: E

TREMOLO BAR: The pitch of the note or chord is dropped a specified number of steps then returned to the original pitch.

trem. bar

PALM MUTING: The note is partially muted by the right hand lightly touching the string(s) just before the bridge.

P.M.

MUFFLED STRINGS: A percussive sound is produced by laying the left hand across the strings without depressing them and striking them with the right hand.

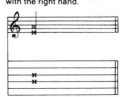

RHYTHM SLASHES: Strum chords in rhythm indicated. Use chord voicings found in the fingering diagrams at the top of the first page of the transcription.

Am   D

RHYTHM SLASHES (SINGLE NOTES): Single notes can be indicated in rhythm slashes. The circled number above the note name indicates which string to play. When successive notes are played on the same string, only the fret numbers are given.

⑤3fr.   2fr.   open   ⑥3fr.
C   B   A   G